Original title:
Echoes of the Sea Life

Copyright © 2025 Creative Arts Management OÜ
All rights reserved.

Author: Harrison Blake
ISBN HARDBACK: 978-1-80587-432-4
ISBN PAPERBACK: 978-1-80587-902-2

Beneath the Ocean's Veil

Down below where fish all swim,
They wiggle and giggle, a lively hymn.
Octopus is juggling, what a sight,
While crabs do the cha-cha, quite tonight.

Seahorses sip on algae tea,
Sardines form a band, just wait and see.
Starfish are sunbathing on the floor,
While herring tell tales of days of yore.

Tranquil Murmurs in Blue

In the calm of waves, a turtle glides,
Wearing a bowtie, it laughs and rides.
Clownfish are practicing a new routine,
Doing the tango with grace quite keen.

Dolphins leap high, they dance with glee,
Spinning and whirling, just wait for me!
With a splash and a dash, they pass by fast,
In this underwater party, fun unsurpassed.

The Lure of the Siren's Song

A siren sings with a voice so sweet,
But her fishy friends don't want to greet.
They cover their ears, say 'not again!'
She'll lure the sailors, but they're all men.

Her seaweed hair flows with laughter loud,
While all the turtles form a giggling crowd.
She sneezes a tune, bubbles fill the air,
Critters all snicker, they haven't a care.

Tales of the Tidal Pool

In a tide pool's splash, the sea urchins chat,
Planning a party—imagine that!
Anemones sway to the beat of the tide,
While barnacles gossip, side by side.

The hermit crabs scurry, shells all aglow,
Debating the best place to dance and show.
Weird creatures gather 'neath starry skies,
In this wacky world, there's laughter and sighs.

Reflections on the Ocean Floor

Bubbles rise with giggles loud,
A crab dancing, oh so proud!
Fish trade secrets with a wink,
Jellyfish join in with a jink.

Seashells gossip, sharing tales,
Starfish laughing, no need for scales.
Turtles chuckle, spinning round,
Finding joy where snails abound.

Chants of the Nautical Night

Mermaids tease with winking eyes,
Singing songs that make waves rise.
Octopus grabs the mic with flair,
His eight hands dance, a seaweed hair.

Sea cucumbers, quite the jest,
Telling jokes, they think they're best.
Dolphins giggle, flip and dive,
In the moonlight, all come alive.

The Silent Call of the Deep

Whales whisper soft, a funny rhyme,
Sharing jokes from olden time.
Anemones wave, giving high fives,
While fish in hats do improv lives.

Clownfish chuckle, what a sight,
Dancing around, with pure delight.
Coral reefs with vibrant flair,
Host a party, without a care.

Melodies of the Moonlit Shore

Sand crabs slide, they breakdance free,
What a spectacle, come and see!
Seagulls squawk, a raucous choir,
The beach's vibe grows ever higher.

With each wave, a splash of fun,
Starfish playing, never done.
The tide rolls in, a laughter tide,
Where ocean friends all abide.

Rippling Reveries

Bubbles giggle and dance, oh so spry,
As crabs do the cha-cha, waving goodbye.
Seashells whisper tales with a twinkling sound,
Nautilus parade through the kelp battleground.

Clownfish wear smiles in playful disguise,
While starfish are busy, just counting the ties.
A dolphin does flips, with a splash and a grin,
"It's a party down here, let the fun truly begin!"

Ballet of the Breaching Whales

Whales hold a gala with grand pirouettes,
Splashing around in their wobbly sets.
With tails like confetti, they leap and they whirl,
Keeping the fish on their tippy-toe swirl.

"Two for the price of one!" they quip with delight,
As a seagull observes, with a roguish flight.
"Can you believe this? The water's our stage!"
The fish cheer them on, "You've outdone every age!"

The Stillness Beneath the Swell

Underneath the waves, where the seaweed can sway,
A flatfish plays hide and seek all day.
"Oy! Where'd you go?" calls the innocent crab,
"No idea!" laughs flatfish, "Guess I'm a fab!"

A turtle in slow-mo, determined and wise,
Says, "I'm almost there—oh, look at those fries!"
With jellyfish floaty, in a gooey ballet,
They giggle and wobble, in their jellyfish array.

Waters That Speak

In waters that chatter, with gurgles and burbles,
A fish tells a story of snacks and of grumbles.
"Hey, did you hear? The shrimp hold a feast!
But watch out for the octopus; he's quite the beast!"

Anemones nod, all fuzzy and bright,
As they sway and they sway, what a curious sight!
The seahorses joke, "Time for a dance-off!"
While the waves laugh aloud, "We're the coolest, off we scoff!"

Gerrymandered Currents

Fish swim in circles, what a sight,
Chasing their tails, they take flight.
A crab with a wig claims to be chic,
While octopuses plot, arguing technique.

Seagulls dive down, making a fuss,
Stealing the snacks, oh what a plus!
The waves laugh softly, they know the game,
"Catch us if you can!" they shout without shame.

The Lament of the Abandoned Dock

Once a proud place, now rust and decay,
A lonely old plank complains every day.
The barnacles gossip, they cling and they cling,
While a tired old buoy makes a sad ping.

A fish in a tux dreams of champagne,
But all he can find is some seaweed grain.
Crabby old guests tell tales from the past,
Of parties and laughter that didn't last.

Breeze-Borne Secrets of the Harbor

Whispers of dolphins wearing bow ties,
Waltzing with mermaids under the skies.
A pelican sings with a voice like a cat,
While turtles roll over, "What's up with that?"

The wind carries jokes from the shore to the tide,
Where plankton groove, with nowhere to hide.
Fish throw a dance party, the catch of the day,
All while the seagulls try to ballet.

The Language of the Salted Waves

Waves tickle the shore, giggling away,
They bounce off the rocks and start to play.
A starfish on point, strikes a pose,
While clams keep it zen, with eyes like a prose.

The lighthouse grins, standing tall and bright,
While sea cucumbers dance into the night.
"Is this considered a date?" a crab asks with glee,
As barnacles roll their eyes, "Just let it be!"

Whirlpools of Time and Memory

In a whirlpool, fish take a spin,
With seashells clapping, they start to grin.
The octopus dances, what a sight,
While crabs break out in a comical fight.

A starfish attempts to juggle a clam,
But ends up just being a sea's best jam.
Turtles gossip about the last tide,
While dolphins giggle, their joy hard to hide.

Sonatas of the Squid's Plight

A squid with a flair for the dramatic,
Plays the sea like a grand piano, aquatic.
With ink as the notes, he writes silly tunes,
As the fish hum along, beneath laughing moons.

Goby fish tap dance on coral so bright,
While seaweed sways, feeling the night.
The grumpy old snail, he's groaning with glee,
As the octopus oinks, quite happy to be free.

Beneath the Surface: A Forgotten Chorus

Beneath the waves, there's a jolly band,
With sea urchins strumming, quite out of hand.
Anemones sway with rhythm and flair,
As fishy performers swim everywhere.

A lionfish prances, so proud and so bright,
While goofy old turtles keep missing their flight.
The pelicans chuckle at poor crabs in bowls,
As sea cucumbers roll, losing their souls.

The Rhythm of the Roiling Waters

The waters dance wildly, with bursts of glee,
While hermit crabs chirp in a playful spree.
The shells keep the beat with a clattering sound,
As jellyfish glide, twirling round and round.

Clownfish are laughing, a big show they make,
Who knew that a sea can be one big flake?
While waves whisper secrets, all bubbles and froth,
The telegraph crabs send "ha-ha" with cloth.

Twilight at the Waters' Edge

The crab wears a hat made of shell,
Sipping the sea breeze, oh what a swell!
A fish with a pipe down in his fin,
Playing jazz tunes, let the fun begin!

The gulls are rehearsing their comedy act,
Dropping their food, oh that's a bad fact!
The sun dips low, with a wink and a grin,
As starfish dance, they're sure to win!

Chorus of the Sea Creatures

With a splash and a clap, the dolphins play,
Telling each other, 'Hey, I swam this way!'
The clams start to giggle, they can't take a break,
While sea cucumbers shake like a flake!

The octopus juggles some seashells with flair,
Saying, 'How many arms does it take to care?'
The jellyfish float, with a glow and a float,
Hey, are those vibes, or did someone just gloat?

Remnants of the Raging Tide

The seashells are scattered and part of the joke,
As seagulls all squawk, but they sometimes choke!
A walrus slips in, with a splash and a roar,
Saying, 'Watch me high dive, you'll all want to score!'

Starfish debate on who wore it best,
'It's me!' shouts one, with a spiky chest.
As the tide rolls back, what a sight to see,
Anemones laugh, all in glee, whee!

A Journey through Aquatic Melodies

The seaweed sways like it's Gatsby's dance,
Crabs in tuxedos, giving love a chance.
Fishes in bow ties swim twirling around,
A party down here, the best ever found!

The barnacles hum a tune of delight,
Swaying intertwined through the softening night.
As waves clap along, and bubbles pop too,
You'll find a sea party, just waiting for you!

Murmurs Beneath the Waves

Fish chat with a splash, so bright,
Crabs leg wrestle in the twilight.
Seashells gossip, spin tall tales,
While starfish search for their missing scales.

Jellyfish dance with wobbly grace,
As shrimp throw parties, a wild embrace.
Octopuses juggle with eight arms wide,
In the aquatic circus, they take great pride.

Reflections in Saltwater

The seaweed wiggles, it tickles the toes,
When dolphins play tag and everyone knows.
A pelican drops a fish, what a catch!
But ends up with seaweed, a slimy patch!

Waves pull pranks, splash joy all around,
As clams play the music, with shells they've found.
The jellybeans tumble through bubbles in style,
Calling all fish for a glittery smile.

Songs of the Underwater Realm

Crabs sing ballads in their sandy halls,
While snappy seals ring in their calls.
A whale drops a beat with a bassy boom,
As fish fish for fame in the coral's room.

Starfish strut like they're on a stage,
Winking at turtles, turning the page.
Anemones sway with their colorful swirls,
In a dance party of oceanic pearls.

Sirens of the Deep

Mermaids giggle over clams, oh dear,
While sea turtles roll with laughter and cheer.
A crab wearing glasses reads underwater news,
While flounders flip-flop in their funny shoes.

Sea otters juggle with rocks in delight,
While squids share stories late into the night.
Abalone fashion shows, they strut and preen,
In the zany world of seaweed cuisine.

Symphony of Aquatic Life

In coral reefs, a fish parade,
Bubbles dance, a joyful charade.
Clownfish joke, with anemone friend,
Underwater giggles that never end.

A dolphin dives, a splashy sight,
Jellyfish float in a colorful flight.
A crab with swagger walks sideways slow,
While starfish cheer from the ocean's glow.

Turtles glide with a graceful ease,
Playing tag with the swinging sea-weez.
Octopuses juggle with eight-armed flair,
Cracking jokes with saltwater air.

An underwater band begins to play,
With seashells drumming in rhythmic sway.
Every fish joins with a joyful glee,
In this silly aquatic jubilee!

The Unwritten Code of the Waves

A fish in bowtie goes on a date,
With seaweed snacks on a clam-shaped plate.
But it's hard to flirt when you can't say much,
Just wave hello with a gentle touch.

A lobster's wearing its red-hot news,
Spreading gossip like morning blues.
"Did you hear about the starfish's new dress?
Oh my, it's not good, I have to confess!"

Seagulls squawk with a laugh and a tease,
Over fishermen searching for their big keys.
While fish hide in rocks, enjoying the show,
Mollusks whisper, "Let's keep it on the low!"

A crab says, "Rules? Not us for sure!"
"Let's just have fun; that's the ocean's lure!"
With laughter echoed in foamy delight,
The waves just giggle, it's a funny sight!

Embrace of the Ocean's Calm

A pufferfish holds a yoga class,
Stretching fins while dolphins pass.
"Breathe in deep, let the tension go,
Oh, look, a whale just joined the show!"

Crabs in their suits practice a pose,
As sea turtles contemplate their flows.
"Namaste," they say, with heartfelt glee,
Finding peace in their watery spree.

The waves roll gently, like a soft lullaby,
As fishes giggle and do a fly-by.
Starfish meditate, just splashing about,
While squids juggle just to show off and shout!

"Remember," says shark, "to enjoy the ride,
Life's too short, let's swim with pride!"
With fins in the air and smiles all around,
In the calm of the ocean, joy can be found!

Tales Carried by the Current

A fish in a hat, what a sight,
Told jokes to the crabs, full of delight.
They laughed 'til they splashed, what a scene,
In bubbles of giggles, the sea so keen.

The turtle wore shades, oh so cool,
Skimming the waves like a brand-new fool.
A starfish danced on the ocean floor,
While a clam snapped shut, yelling, "No more!"

Ripples of Forgotten Dreams

A jellyfish floated with style so grand,
Waving its tentacles like a band.
Said, "Hey, watch my moves! Isn't it neat?"
The sardines all cheered, tapping their feet.

A dolphin, with flair, jumped through the air,
Cracking a joke that made the sea stare.
"Why did the crab not share its prize?"
"Because it was shell-fish!"—the truth in disguise.

Voices of the Undersea Wind

An octopus painted his room quite bright,
With colors and patterns, oh what a sight!
Said, "Who needs brushes when you've got arms?"
And swirled the sea with artistic charms.

A clam opened up, sharing a laugh,
Said, "Let's tell a story about a giraffe!"
The fish all looked puzzled, they just couldn't see,
How a long-necked beast could relate to the sea!

Harmonies of the Marine Depths

A walrus sang in the key of a whale,
Rhyming with bubbles, leaving a trail.
The anemones swayed to the funny beat,
As seahorses danced with their own little feet.

Yet, the pufferfish puffed, full of pride,
Said, "I'm the balloon of the ocean tide!"
But with one little poke, it flopped to the floor,
Telling the sea, "Hey, I can't take much more!"

Dances of the Wandering Fishes

In bright hula skirts, they prance,
With fins that twirl in a fishy dance.
Bubbles pop like a dance floor beat,
With crabs doing the two-step, oh so neat!

They shimmy past coral, bright and bold,
In a party that never gets old.
Clams can't clap, but they sure do cheer,
For every fish that swims near here!

Secrets of the Surging Tide

Whispers of waves tickle the shore,
Seagulls laugh, wanting more.
Each wave rolls in like a pranky tease,
Bringing lost socks and playful breeze.

The tide plays tricks, it's not a bore,
Hiding treasures, wet and sore.
Starfish giggle, and flip around,
While crabby pals insist they're crowned!

Lullabies from the Aquatic Realm

The octopus sings a crooning song,
Corals sway like they belong.
Fish float by, wide-eyed and keen,
Wondering if they should join the scene.

Jellyfish jiggle, oh so slow,
Twinkling lights in a gentle show.
Even the seaweed sways with delight,
As bubbles hum through the soft moonlight.

Shadows of the Sunken Ship

There's a ship beneath that lost its way,
Hosting parties every day.
Fish organize a treasure hunt,
While barnacles form a clammy front.

The captain's hat is quite the prize,
Worn by a grouper with googly eyes.
Mermaids giggle, giving a shout,
"Let's dance, let's twirl, let's twist about!"

Driftwood Remnants

On the beach, I found a shoe,
Seen better days, it once was blue.
Dancing crabs give it a nudge,
Saying, "Come on, let's not judge!"

A stick that once was proud and tall,
Now used as a make-do wall.
Seagulls laugh, they have no shame,
Saying, "Look, we're all the same!"

Cerulean Reveries

In waves that tickle toes and feet,
A fish made friends, it's quite the feat.
Whale calls sound like a honking horn,
Fish giggle, 'Oh, how we've sworn!'

The seaweed wraps like party hats,
Bobbing with joy, it dances with sprats.
Starfish chill with a wink and grin,
Counting tales they've pulled from fin.

The Secrets of Sand and Surf

Sandcastles rise, then tumble down,
As children giggle, sporting a crown.
Shells telling tales of their great struggle,
Fighting tides—life's a lovely muddle!

A starfish murmurs, 'I'll find my way,'
As crabs dance by in a graceful sway.
Seashells gossip about the breeze,
While jellyfish floats with such calm ease.

Beneath the Surface: A Narrative

Snorkeling wonders, fish in a row,
With clownfish strutting, putting on a show.
Octopus hides with eight arms twirling,
While sea turtles glide, gently swirling.

Bubbles rise, they float like dreams,
As dolphins jump through sunlight beams.
Deep down, a party's going strong,
Underwater dance, they all belong!

Ghost Stories of the Bay

In the bay where seagulls squawk,
Ghost crabs tell time on a dock.
Fish in tuxedos dance and prance,
While octopuses waltz in a trance.

A clam once whispered to a star,
'You're shining brighter than my car!'
Shrimps giggled, tails in a twist,
As mermaids chuckled, 'Did you get missed?'

A lobster's tale of lost romance,
With a giant squid in a silly dance.
The waves, they chuckle, high and low,
As dolphins swim with a joyous show.

At midnight, the moon flips a coin,
And crabs break out to sing a groin.
The ghost stories swirl through the night,
With laughter echoed, what a sight!

Serenade of the Unseen Creatures

Beneath waves, where the sun won't peek,
Fish hold concerts, play hide-and-seek.
A pufferfish sings off-key,
While jellyfish glow in harmony.

Starfish gather for a rockin' jam,
With sea cucumbers clapping, 'Wham, bam!'
A narwhal strums his magical horn,
As crabs tap dance until they're worn.

The eels groove, twisted in glee,
While plankton sprinkle confetti, whee!
Octopuses juggle shells in a swirl,
In this undersea party, they twirl.

So next time you take a dive in blue,
Listen closely for the sounds anew.
The ocean's singing, who knew it could?
With fins and flippers, feeling so good!

The Tide's Lament

Oh, tide, you're lazy, take a break,
Waves crash down, for goodness' sake!
The crab declares, 'I need some sun!'
As the fish laugh, 'This isn't fun!'

A clam retorts, 'Don't be a pest!'
While barnacles cling and get some rest.
The turtled ancients sigh and say,
'I swear, it's slower every day!'

The whale complains of being too big,
Squeezed in a wriggly, squishy gig.
But the starfish brushes off the gloom,
Saying, 'The tide will swing back, vroom!'

So dance with the waves, oh weary sea,
Join in the laughter, wild and free.
For tides may wane, but don't you fret,
There's always more fun, just don't forget!

Voyage of the Deep Blue

Take a boat on the ocean wide,
Sail with the fishes, feel the tide.
A crab as captain, what a sight,
Waving his claws, ready for flight.

The gulls squawk jokes from up above,
While dolphins perform with lots of love.
The octopus steers with all eight hands,
Keeping the crew strong with his plans.

But what's this? A whale with a song?
Belly flops, singing all night long!
The mermaids giggle, splashing about,
'We're sailing to laughter, no doubt!'

So come aboard this silly ship,
With fishy tales that make you flip.
The sea may be deep, but don't you sigh,
With friends like these, the fun won't die!

Murmurs of the Rock Pools

In the rock pools, crabs do prance,
With wobbly moves, they take a chance.
A fish slips by, says, "Hey, it's me!"
"I need to swim, not do the spree!"

An octopus sneezes, squirts some ink,
The seaweed giggles, what do you think?
Starfish sit up, looking quite fine,
"Maybe it's time we all drank some brine!"

Clams share stories of their wild dates,
"Last week, a mussel tried to pry my gates!"
Laughter rings out as waves do roll,
While snails compete to reach the shore's shoal.

A seagull flies by, with a snack so grand,
"Who knew chips could be so unplanned?"
The tide rolls in, with a splishy-splash,
"Hold onto your shells, it's time for a splash!"

Hymn of the Sailor's Heart

A sailor sings to the salty breeze,
His voice cracks, but he does as he please.
"Where's my rum?" he shouts with glee,
Then trips on a net, oh, woe is he!

With fishy friends and jellybean dreams,
He steers his boat while giggling in streams.
A dolphin pops up, with a flip and a dive,
"What's happening here? I'm shocked you're alive!"

Seagulls squawk jokes, oh what a delight,
"Why do pirates only take to the night?"
They cackle and glide, all over his head,
"Because they can't get caught, in daylight, they're dead!"

The waves join the fun, with a frothy cheer,
"Oops, there goes your hat, now that's quite clear!"
The sailor holds tight to his one-legged peg,
It's a funny old life; still, he won't beg!

The Ocean's Lost Conversations

Crabs whisper secrets in sandy halls,
While fish gossip, swimming through coral walls.
"Did you hear that? A tuna got stung!"
"Oh no, not again! That's really not fun!"

A clam argues loudly with a stubborn shrimp,
"I swear I saw a dolphin, it just did a flip!"
But the shrimp rolls his eyes, quite set in his ways,
"Just let it go, it's just a phase!"

Walruses chuckle in a deep, goofy tone,
"Where's the best spot to find a big bone?"
They swap potluck recipes, written in algae,
"Trust me, it tastes better than old soggy!"

Turtles slow dance, basking in sun,
While laughing at fish who think they can run.
"Race us?" they shout, "Bet you won't win!"
But the fish scoff back, "You're too slow to begin!"

Voices Carried by the Breezes

Upon the cliffs, the gulls take flight,
Chasing each other in a comical sight.
"Why did the crab cross the sandy lane?"
"Because the ocean called out, 'It's no use in vain!'"

The wind carries whispers from distant shores,
Waves chime in, offering lively roars.
"Let's have a party beneath the full moon!"
"Just watch out for the waves, they'll make you swoon!"

A school of fish plays hide and seek,
"Can you find me?" they giggle, trying to sneak.
But alas, the bigger fish just notice their flair,
And one says, "Guys, you've got scales to spare!"

Seashells gossip, spinning tall tales,
Of storms and sailors and fanciful gales.
"Last week, I saw a ship sink and float!"
"More like you dreamed riding a goat!"

Nautical Reverberations

The fish wear hats, all quite absurd,
A crab sings high, we all just heard.
Seagulls laugh as they dive and swoop,
The octopus joins in, starts a loop.

A whale tries to dance, oh what a sight,
Trips on a wave, oh what a fright!
Turtles are giggling, under the sun,
While jellyfish twirl - they're having fun!

The shrimp play cards in their sandy homes,
While starfish decorate in glossy chrome.
A dolphin tells jokes, all day it seems,
While barnacles dream in their quirky dreams.

Under the waves, a party's alive,
With creatures of all kinds - a finned hive!
Tonight we feast on seaweed and glee,
In this wacky world, come join, you'll see!

Where Stars Meet the Ocean

The starfish kept saying, 'We're better than you!',
While dolphins just laughed, 'That ain't true!'
Bubbles of laughter filled the blue sea,
As sardines swam by with a dance and a spree.

Anemones blush with the tide's gentle kiss,
While clams clap their shells, they can't help but hiss.
A whale in a tux, very dapper, so neat,
Whispers to crabs, 'Check out my beat!'

The moon casts a grin, shining bright overhead,
As octopuses juggle, their nightly bread.
With forks and with spoons, the squid set the scene,
While sea cucumbers clean up the green.

In this waltz of the waves, they sing and they swirl,
While seahorses ride in a dizzying whirl.
A party of misfits, with humor galore,
The night spills laughter from ocean's own floor!

A Symphony of Waves

The tide rolls in, and the seafoam giggles,
As dolphins play tag, dance, twist, and wiggle.
Clownfish parade in their stripes of bright hue,
While lobsters stand guard, all tough and askew.

Seaweed sways gently, waving in tune,
Mermaids are laughing, their hair's a festoon.
A conch shell horn plays a whimsical song,
While the fish in the coral all sing along.

Shrimps in a conga line, marching with pride,
Seashells stack high, the ocean's own guide.
Starfish throw confetti, all colors they bear,
As the tide carries on, without a single care.

A seal does a backflip, the crowd goes wild,
Even sea urchins join in, oh how they smiled!
Together they swell in a joyful parade,
In the symphony made where mischief's displayed!

Driftwood Diaries

A piece of driftwood has tales to spin,
Of crabs in tuxedos who dance with a grin.
A school of fish stoked up a wild bet,
Who'd swim the fastest - what a silly set!

The seagulls took notes, with tiny green pens,
Recording the gossip of fishy best friends.
A clam tells the news, crack it open with glee,
While surf's rolling in, sipping salty tea.

A hermit crab wanders, wearing a shoe,
Searching for shells that sparkled anew.
Starfish share secrets, with color ablaze,
As the ocean chuckles in a salty haze.

So gather your driftwood, join in this tale,
Of fishy friendships that never grow stale.
For in the grand depths where joy knows no bounds,
It's laughter and stories that truly resounds!

Whispers of the Tidal Breeze

Crabs in tuxedos, dance with glee,
Tickling fish that's fancy free.
Seagulls squawking, quite the show,
Wave their wings, in bright sun glow.

Jellyfish flash like disco lights,
Dancing beneath the moonlit nights.
Starfish stuck on a merry spree,
Sharing secrets, just you and me.

Clams and oysters play hide and seek,
Counting bubbles, it's quite a feat!
Octopus joins, wearing a hat,
"Oh, what a party," says the chatty brat!

Dolphins giggle, do flips and dives,
While seaweed sways, oh how it thrives.
A playful splash, and all lose track,
Of who's the funniest in this pack!

Murmurs Beneath the Waves

A shrimp plays spoons, what a sight,
Clams are rapping, full of delight.
The anemones sway to the beat,
Inviting everyone for a seat.

Turtles wearing glasses, how absurd,
Caught up in chasing a silly bird.
Fish in bow ties, oh what a fuss,
Throwing a party just for us!

Sardines whisper a fishy joke,
'What did the clam say to the bloke?'
All the sea stars laugh out loud,
In their sparkling smiles, they are proud.

Eels doing limbo, oh what fun!
Bubbles popping, the dance has begun.
Amidst soft whispers of tides, we cheer,
Who knew the ocean could be so dear?

Ghosts of the Coral Reef

Coral ghosts in colorful hue,
Waltzing together, not one or two.
They giggle as fish zoom by,
'Oh, don't scare us!' they seem to cry.

A parrotfish, with a feathered hat,
Tells tall tales, imagine that!
Ghouls of the reef, a comedic bunch,
Sharing tales over a coral lunch.

Manta rays glide, with grace and flair,
"Did you see that? He split the air!"
With ghostly laughs and jokes galore,
Underwater mischief forevermore.

In this haunted, colorful gleam,
A party unfolds, more than a dream.
Between the laughs, an aquatic cheer,
Not your average spook, that's quite clear!

Songs in the Saltwater

Sandy toes and salty air,
Crabs tap dance without a care.
Fish sing tunes with plucky voices,
In the ocean, everyone rejoices!

Walrus choir in a concert hall,
"Don't forget to invite your pals!"
Seahorses trot in their fancy shoes,
"Dance with us, you cannot lose!"

Anemones swaying in sweet delight,
As jellyfish glow, oh what a sight.
With sea cucumbers shaking a tail,
They gather round for the next big tale.

From the shallows to the reefs so deep,
The songs carry on, never to sleep.
In this salty world, laughter and cheer,
Join the chorus, let's all persevere!

Ballad of the Echoing Conch

A conch tells tales with each loud pop,
Of fishy meetings and a humor drop.
A crustacean danced, slipped on a shell,
And all the sea laughed; oh, what a swell!

A school of fish in bright parade,
Said, "Hey, watch this! Let's make a shade!"
They swam in circles, a dizzy sight,
Each flip and flop brought pure delight.

A crab once tried to take a leap,
But landed on a clam—oh dear, so deep!
With a clang and clatter, laughter spread,
As seabirds laughed, "Uncle Crab, well bred!"

So if you stroll along the sand,
Listen closely, as creatures band.
In the salty laughter, joy breaks free,
For life beneath the waves is jolly as can be!

The Symphony of Shimmering Scales

The fish held a concert, scales all aglow,
With bubbles for beats in a watery show.
A guppy on tambourine, small yet spry,
While lobsters snapped claws to the rhythm nearby.

The octopus juggled, what a sight to see!
With jellyfish floating, full of glee.
They all sang together in one big squawk,
Briny ballads only the deep could talk.

The seaweed swayed in a goofy dance,
Even a starfish wanted a chance!
But once it got moving, twirled round and round,
With a wobble and flip, it fell to the ground.

Yet the show went on, a whimsical spree,
As dolphins joined in with their antics, whee!
Underwater giggles filled the deep blue,
And in this mad concert, there was joy anew!

Whispers of Tides

The tide came rolling, a giddy wave,
Chasing shore crabs, oh how they behave!
They scuttled and scampered, a comical race,
With each little splash, they made quite a face.

A sea otter lounged, quite lazy indeed,
Grooming its fur, while munching on seaweed.
It chuckled aloud with a wink and a grin,
Life in the ocean, full of free-spirited win!

Seagulls above played aerial games,
Diving and swooping with silly claims.
One missed its target, oh what a sight!
And landed headfirst in a splash of light.

So if you hear giggles on ocean's face,
It's just the waves having a fun little chase.
For life in the brine is full of delight,
Where laughter and joy take to flight!

Chasing Fathomless Dreams

A squid dreamed big, of a grand ballet,
With lights from above and sea stars at play.
It twirled and it flipped, with such flair to show,
While fish in the front row yelled, "Bravo! Go!"

The clownfish chuckled, in stripes of bright hue,
Joined in the fun with a wild curtsy too.
"We're the jesters of water!" they all did proclaim,
As they floated and jolted, oh what a game!

An eel joined the dance, all slinky and sly,
But tangled in kelp, it let out a sigh.
"Not my best move," it murmured with cheer,
As all of its friends gave a rousing cheer.

In the ocean's vast dreams, one thing is sure,
The laughter is endless, the joy will endure.
With creatures at play, and frolics so grand,
Life in the deep is one funny band!

Whirlpools of Memory

The octopus juggles seashells with flair,
While fish swap their tales without any care.
A dolphin dives deep with a twist and a grin,
A mermaid's lost comb? Just where does it begin?

The crab in a top hat takes center stage,
While seahorses dance, oh, what a parade!
A clam shouts, 'I'm shy!' but it starts to sing,
As waves crash along, we all join the fling.

The barnacles gossip on rocks all day long,
Singing about how they can't get along.
A starfish just laughed, and said with a cheer,
"Life's better with friends and perhaps a cold beer!"

So dwell in the splashes, enjoy all the jest,
Nature's a circus, and we're all impressed.
With bubbles and giggles, the waters delight,
In oceanic fun, we'll stay 'til the night.

Ballads of Marine Life

A pufferfish blows up to look quite round,
While sea turtles glide, without making a sound.
The cod wears a tie to an undersea ball,
And clownfish just chuckle, they're having a ball.

The lobsters throw a party, oh what a sight,
With shrimp salsa dancing till the morning light.
A whale hums a tune that nobody knows,
Whilst anemones sway in their bubbly clothes.

The squid tries to paint, but makes quite a mess,
Colors of chaos in a watery dress.
Near the coral, a seagull lets out a joke,
And the dolphins break into laughter, no smoke.

With a splash and a giggle, the fish join the song,
In this underwater world, where all things belong.
An oyster turns shy, and retracts with a frown,
While the tide keeps on rolling through this bustling town.

The Echoing Sands

The sand crab wears shades and strolls down the shore,
While the gulls squawk a tune that we can't ignore.
A starfish on land says, "Hey, I'm still cool!"
While sea cucumbers play leapfrog in the pool.

The shells tell their stories in whispers so sweet,
Of fishy romances in the waves where they meet.
A sea lion rolls in the sun, taking a nap,
Dreams of sardines in a fanciful trap.

The waves flip and flounder, telling their jokes,
As crabs gather round, all amused by the hoax.
"Don't flip me over," a clam starts to plea,
"I'm more than a plate, can't you just let me be?"

With laughter and shells, the tide comes alive,
As the ocean's own chorus seems eager to thrive.
In swirling sands, life's humor we find,
Where memories swim and adventure's unconfined.

Whispers in the Currents

A fish on a bike rides the currents with glee,
While a snail races past, "You can't catch me!"
A heron drops pizza, takes flight in surprise,
As fishes roll over, discussing their fries.

The currents hum ballads of travel and fun,
As jellyfish twirl, flashing light like the sun.
An eel tells a tale of a lost treasure chest,
While turtles nod along, their knowledge's the best.

A group of dolphins wear sunglasses and hats,
Playing beach volleyball against plump little krabs.
A shrimp cracks a pun, and the laughter subsides,
With bubbles and banter, as happiness rides.

So plunge into waters where joy never ends,
In the melody of life, every creature's your friend.
The ocean's a party, with waves that delight,
Beneath skies of blue and the sparkles of light.

The Chronicles of Distant Shores

A crab in a tuxedo danced with flair,
He slipped on a jellyfish, fell through the air!
A fish with a mustache told jokes at the bar,
While seaweed swayed like a strange bouquet star.

The starfish held court, a crab as the jester,
They laughed till their shells couldn't hold a lester.
A clam offered pearls, but they sparkled too bright,
And dazzled the dolphins, who danced with delight.

With sea cucumbers playing the maracas,
They hosted a party that baffled the walruses.
The mermaids sang tunes with a wobbly twist,
Their notes causing giggles from fish in the mist.

So if you find shores with a whiff of whimsy,
Just follow the giggles, it's sure to be flimsy.
For life in the tide is a circus, it seems,
With silly fish prancing and chasing their dreams.

Secrets of the Briny Depths

There once was a dolphin who loved to tell tales,
He claimed that he rode on a ship with big sails.
But all of his friends just rolled over in glee,
They knew he was fishy; he just swam for free!

A turtle named Larry wore glasses quite thick,
He read all the maps, but got lost on the lick.
"Oh dear," said the octopus, flipping a page,
"Your navigational skills are far from sage!"

The plankton would gossip about crabs in disguise,
Saying, "A pinch from them would be quite a surprise!"
While shrimps held a rally, all marching in line,
They planned a parade with a coconut shrine.

So down in the depths, where the silliness flows,
The laughter ignites, and the mirth often grows.
For secrets of oceans are better when shared,
With tales of the strange, how treasures unpaired!

Lullabies from the Deep Blue

A sleepy seahorse hummed soft in the night,
While a whale tickled fishes, what a curious sight!
The corals turned pink with a giggly hue,
As clownfish performed in their bright rainbow crew.

An octopus knits with its colorful yarn,
It hooks up a blanket made from seaweed and barn.
The sea stars sang softly, a dreamy ballet,
As bubbles bubbled up, taking worries away.

The mermaids cooed sweetly, their tails all aglow,
With stories of pirates who danced to and fro.
The sand below shimmered with laughter and cheer,
As every sea creature lent an ear near.

So if you are drifting on tides of the blue,
Remember the lullabies whispered, it's true.
For even in waters where silence may creep,
The fun never fades, it just swims off to sleep.

The Heartbeat of the Ocean

In depths where the giggles bubble and boil,
A clam wearing sneakers shares tales that uncoil.
He tells of a lobster with a great sense of pride,
Who wore a tuxedo and danced with a slide.

The sea urchins chuckled, a spiky affair,
As turtles did cartwheels without much of a care.
A school of fish giggled while swimming in packs,
Their scales flashed like sequins, with jazzy knickknacks.

A seagull flew down, with a canvas of dreams,
Painting pictures of jellybeans bursting at seams.
The sunbeams would dance on the surface so bright,
Chasing shadows and giddy, inviting the night.

So tune in to waves and their rhythmic delight,
For laughter is carried on currents of light.
In the heartbeat of waters, the joy's ever bold,
With creatures of seascape, and stories retold.

Voices from the Abyss

Fishtales and mermaids, oh what a sight,
Dancing in the currents, day turns to night.
Crabs join the party, tapping their claws,
Singing with dolphins, it's never a pause.

Octopus with a hat, a sight so absurd,
Recites all the gossip, not one word unheard.
Starfish spinning yarns, all in good fun,
While turtles nod along, not missing a pun.

Whales crack the jokes, deep in the blue,
With laughter like thunder, a playful crew.
The jellyfish jiggle, glowing so bright,
As fish giggle softly, in sheer delight.

But when the tidal wave comes rolling in,
All scatter and hide, just like old kin.
Except for the clam, who won't budge an inch,
Claiming he's the star, while others just flinch.

Currents of Forgotten Tales

The anchor's a relic, lost long ago,
Swallowed by seaweed, all covered in glow.
The seagulls are squawking, trolling for lunch,
As crabs throw a barbecue, oh what a munch!

Barnacles gossip, stuck on the hull,
Telling tall tales that are always a bull.
The pufferfish sighs, 'I just want to play,'
While the sea cucumbers groove, keeping the sway.

An old pirate's ghost, with a frown on his face,
Looks for his treasure, lost in this place.
The minnows all giggle, enjoying the show,
As waves keep on rolling, in bubbly flow.

Mermaids throw parties with shells as their cups,
While otters compete in the silliest ups.
Together they laugh as the tides ebb and flow,
In the currents of stories, all full of glow.

Beneath the Shell's Resonate

Under the surface, where the fun never stops,
Creatures of mischief play musical flops.
Conch shells are trumpets, making a ruckus,
While clownfish perform, in bright clownish focus.

The shrimp start a conga, with seahorses behind,
Each twist and turn, a jumbled unwind.
The seaweed joins in, swaying with glee,
As bubbles pop loudly, like they're in a spree.

Corals all cheer for the jellyfish queen,
Who sways and glows in the disco-like scene.
'Come dance with the tide!' the starfish all shout,
As they shimmy and laugh, in a watery bout.

But who gets the last laugh? The crab with a grin,
As he hoards all the snacks, knuckles drawn in.
With a clink of his shell, the night's ending soon,
And sea creatures sigh, under the sly moon.

The Language of Water

Water's a chatterbox, gurgling away,
Sharing funny tales from the ocean's ballet.
With splashes and swirls, it tells of the fun,
Of fish playing tag, just trying to run.

The seaweed rolls laughter, like waves in a breeze,
While the clams keep it secret beneath the tall trees.
Turtles are gossiping, slow and quite wise,
As shrimps dash around, with their elaborate lies.

Saltwater whispers the jokes of the day,
As anemones tickle, in their own quirky way.
Each ripple a chuckle, each wave a bright jest,
In the depths of the blue, the sea's always blessed.

So dive into laughter, let the pearls swing free,
In this salty abode, where all creatures agree.
For in every splash, and in every fun dart,
Lies the joyful refrain of the oceanic heart.

Legends of the Deep

There once was a mermaid named Lou,
With a shell hat as bright as the dew.
She danced with the fish,
In a watery swish,
And sang off-key tunes just for you.

A crab tried to pinch her long hair,
But she giggled and said, "I don't care!"
He slipped on a clam,
With a loud, silly slam,
And they laughed till they gasped for fresh air.

The octopus played poker at night,
And cheated, though it wasn't quite right.
He'd wink with a tentacle,
In a game so hysterical,
Leaving fishy friends feeling slighted.

In the end, they all forged a pact,
To celebrate laughter, no act.
With bubbles and glee,
Their own jamboree,
In the world where the absurd is intact.

Mysteries of the Ocean's Whisper

A dolphin who loved silly tricks,
Danced on the waves like a flick.
But when he took flight,
And landed in fright,
He splashed all the seals, oh what a mix!

A sea turtle claimed to be fast,
But with each little push, he fell last.
He raced with the breeze,
But grazed seaweed trees,
His dreams of speed turned to contrast.

A starfish who dreamt of the shore,
Tried crawling, but fell with a roar.
He flipped on his back,
In a wobbly act,
Saying, "I'm destined for so much more!"

In this world beneath the bright sun,
Each creature found ways to have fun.
With giggles and games,
And silly old names,
Life's a splash when they all come undone.

The Haunting of Forgotten Coastlines

There once was a ghostly old whale,
Who washed up with a spine made of shale.
He moaned in the night,
In a comical fright,
Scaring all lobsters, they turned pale!

A pirate with socks made of seaweed,
Claimed treasure that none ever need.
He'd sing out in glee,
'This booty's for me!'
Though all he had was a lost seed.

The barnacles played peek-a-boo,
Sticking out from a sunken canoe.
They winked with a grin,
As fish tried to swim,
Each giggle made the waves feel anew.

At the break of each dawn, they'd all cheer,
With tales of their goofy career.
In a world so bizarre,
Where the laughter shines far,
The coastlines would echo their cheer.

Splash of Fables

A seahorse who fancied a race,
Wore a saddle and took up the space.
He zoomed past a star,
In his bright, silly car,
Till he slipped on a jellyfish base!

A clam crafted pearls made of cheese,
And served them with crackers and peas.
The fish dined in style,
With laughter and bile,
Claiming, "This feast is sure to please!"

The sea cucumber danced on the floor,
In a tutu, he made quite a score.
With each little twirl,
He gave it a whirl,
Leaving everyone wanting for more!

Thus stories were spun in the waves,
Of furry fish and eccentric knaves.
In the depths of their glee,
Laughter rang free,
And friendship was all that it saves.

Ripples of Ancient Waters

Bubbles rise, fish do prance,
In this watery, wavy dance.
Starfish wearing stylish hats,
Squid with shoes, just like the cats.

Crabs that scuttle in a line,
Clams join in, sipping brine.
Countless critters, all in play,
Soaking sun on a lazy day.

Whales are singing off-key tunes,
Dolphins play like silly loons.
Lobsters leap, in jig they go,
Underwater, a grand show!

Seagulls shout with glee and zest,
Flipping fish, they try their best.
An octopus spins tales of old,
While turtles laugh, brave and bold.

Traces of the Forgotten Sea

Once was a mermaid named Clare,
Who traded fish for the latest hair.
Seashells told of ancient gossip,
But dolphins just rolled their eyes and skipped.

A crab did joke, 'I'm quite the catch!'
While a seahorse scrolled its match.
Barnacles, ancient and wise,
Swapped stories with sparkle in their eyes.

On the sandy shores, a game they played,
Seashells hiding under the shade.
Walruses wearing shades so bright,
Took selfies in the warm sunlight!

With jellyfish glowing, a sight so grand,
They boogied like a funky band.
In this kingdom where laughter roams,
No creature feels far from home!

Reflections on the Ocean's Edge

Perched atop a rock so high,
A seagull winked and dared to fly.
Fish below had quite a chat,
As a dolphin wore a sunhat.

Starry night, a squid took flight,
Holding a neon disco light.
Crab in shades, dancing with flair,
While turtles tried to comb their hair.

The tide brought tales, fishy and bright,
Starfish sang till the morning light.
With a wink, they shared a snack,
Finding treasures in an old backpack.

Hiccups from a cormorant, loud and clear,
As an otter rolled, full of cheer.
All together in rhythmic glee,
Living it up, oh so carefree!

Songs of Sailors Past

Old sailors grumbled on wooden decks,
Trading tales of fish and wrecks.
But the parrots, bright and bold,
Told stories worth their weight in gold.

A cap'n who thought he was a whale,
Paddled in circles, telling his tale.
With every splash, the crew would laugh,
At ships going nowhere, just having a gaff!

The sea shanties all turned silly,
As fish joined in, quite a frilly.
'Is it time for tea or just some fun?'
Said a clam with a wink, under the sun.

With waves that whispered and tickled toes,
Mermaids danced and struck their poses.
In this lively, silly jive,
Even the fish felt alive!

Soliloquy of the Sandy Shore

A crab with a hat, so proud and so grand,
Struts up and down in the shimmering sand.
He dreams of a march, with a band in the tide,
Where jellyfish waltz, and the otters slide.

Seagulls are gossiping, squawking and screeching,
While clams play charades, their secrets they're teaching.
A conch shell recites, with flair and with grace,
Tales of the beach, in this whimsical place.

Legends Written in Sand and Foam

On a turtle's back with a surfboard so sleek,
He rides through the waves, feeling quite unique.
With a wink and a nod, he shows off his flips,
While fish crowd the shore, cheering loudly in quips.

A lobster in shades, sips bottled-up soda,
Claims he's the king, though no one can afford ya.
"Don't mess with my pinch!" he declares with a cheer,
As the tide takes his throne, he shrugs, "What a year!"

The Heartbeat of the Briny Depths

In the depths of the sea, where the fish hold a rave,
A clownfish is dancing, so silly and brave.
He twirls with the sharks and does spins with the rays,
While seaweed provides the most fashionable praise.

A shrimp with a tie pulls off quite the show,
He juggles the pearls, like a true circus pro.
The octopus laughs, at the antics so bright,
As bubbles rise up, dancing into the night.

Canvas of Distant Horizons

A dolphin in shades dives to catch a few waves,
While the seahorses giggle, playing tag with the caves.
They gallop in circles, so fancy and spry,
Creating a splash, under bright sunny sky.

A starfish named Fred claims he's an artiste,
Painting sunsets on shells, creating quite the feast.
He's world-renowned but never gets the gist,
That his canvas is sand, not a grand ocean mist.